FROM LIGHTNING'S STRIKE

Poems from the Ch'ol Language

FROM LIGHTNING'S STRIKE

Poems by Juana Karen Peñate

Translated from the Ch'ol Language
by Carol Rose Little and Charlotte Friedman

Mayapple Press 2026

Published by   Mayapple Press
362 Chestnut Hill Road
Woodstock, NY 12498
mayapplepress.com

ISBN 978-1-952781-32-2
Library of Congress Number 9781952781322

Cover painting: *On a Rainy Day* by Claude Winn
Photo courtesy of the author, taken at Originaria 2024, Pátzcuaro, Michoacán, Mexico
Book designed and typeset by Judith Kerman in Adobe Caslon Pro

Contents

Introduction

A Wide Aperture

To read the poetry of Juana Karen Peñate is to join her on a sensory voyage into the landscape of southern Mexico and an intrapersonal journey to the wellspring of a poet and woman with deep ancestral Mayan roots. Peñate mines and shapes the complexities of her life into the images and sounds that make up her lyric poetry, offering readers places of respite and beauty, fear and outrage. The poet praises and mourns, protests and questions. Threaded through is the natural world, verdant and soaked with rain, infused with the sharp smell of incense, source of language and power. In these poems, ancestors and spirits co-exist with contemporary migration, domestic abuse, and the deaths of loved ones. Peñate subtly shifts her lens from window to mirror, inviting us to see ourselves more clearly, to feel anew what we may have buried deep inside us.

Background

To get to the poet's house from the United States, you would need to take several flights, a bus, two taxis, then hitch a ride on a co-op pickup truck. From the truck, you would see cornfields cascading down a slope and locals carrying satchels of wood or beans to their homes and stores. Encouraged by her mother to reach beyond the traditional roles of women in the culture, Peñate left Tumbalá, Chiapas, to study law and to teach in other Ch'ol communities. Years later, she returned home and has lived there ever since. She has created a life of robust creativity and spirituality, and, through her work, hopes to inspire other Ch'ol people to draw on and celebrate the many riches of their culture.

Ch'ol is a living Mayan language spoken by a quarter of a million people in southern Mexico as well as diasporic communities across North America. The Mesoamerican Mayan language family, with speakers of at least 6.5 million, comprises some thirty languages, each with its own locality and cultural traditions. The languages are as distinct from one another as English is from German or Spanish.

At the beginning of the pandemic, as the world shut its doors, the opportunity to immerse ourselves in Juana Karen Peñate's poetry presented itself. We worked with the original Ch'ol poems. Peñate often translates her own work into Spanish but admits that those poems often become distinct from the original Ch'ol poems. It is impossible to replicate the sounds of Ch'ol in English (or in Spanish). Its soft m's and ñ's are punctuated by the staccatos of k', ch', and ts'. The frequent apostrophe signifies a glottal stop, a brief cessation of air, or when next to another consonant (e.g., k'), an ejective, a sharper version of the consonant. There is no equivalent in English.

Translation is further complicated by the fact that Ch'ol syntax bears no resemblance to that of English. A Ch'ol word may be made up of many small parts, or morphemes. For example, in the poem "I Am the Alphabet," the single word, *säkjamtyäleloñ* can be broken down as *säk*, bright; *jam*, open; *tyälel*, indicating a process (usually marked with -*ing* in English); and *oñ*, first-person subject. The literal translation of one word is equivalent to many words in English—"I am the bright opening." In the poem, the phrase morphs again to become "bright light of morning."

With each poem, we began with a morpheme-by-morpheme translation, a gloss in linguistics. While far from poetry, these lines gave us a strong foundation from which to work. Each poem required many choices, multiple drafts, often lengthy discussions, and trust in each other's skills and respective intuitions.

The poems in *From Lightning's Strike* were curated from Peñate's second and third collections: *Ipusik'al Matye'lum / Heart of the Wild* (2013) and *Isoñil Ja'al / Dance of the Rain* (2025).

"An intelligent woman who walks lightly through the world"

Peñate's poetry is grounded in an explicitly, assertively relational way of being in the world. Nature is not looked upon or at, and functions neither as metaphor nor symbol. The poet's body/self/language exists in and with nature—physically, dialogically, and reverently. They are bound together. We might think of Gretel Ehrlich's immersion in the landscape of Wyoming in *Solace of Open Spaces* and Camille T. Dungy's words: "I don't understand a way we can be honest about who we are without understanding that we are nature." This is not territory exclusive to women, but Peñate speaks, undeniably, as a woman. Her feminism is evident in the voice, tone, and emotional stance of her poetry. The tone often shifts, indicating a comfort in mutability. Psychically, the speaker positions herself as vulnerable to uncertainty, discomfort, pain. She shares her search for her voice with her readers. This brave exposure is a strength that Peñate, in turn, makes available to her readers.

— Carol Rose Little and Charlotte Friedman

A Guide to Pronunciation of the Ch'ol Alphabet

a — like "**a**" in *father*

ä — like "**e**" in *darkness*

b — like "**b**" in *boy* but said more softly with the breath drawn slightly inward rather than pushed out

ch, ch' —like "**ch**" in *chili*

e — like "**ay**" in *say*

i — like "**ee**" in *see*

j — like "**h**" in *house*

k, k' — like "**k**" in *kite*

l — like "**l**" in *lamp*

m — like "**m**" in *moon*

ñ — like "**ny**" in *canyon* (or Spanish *ñ* in *niño*)

o — like "**o**" in *note*

p, p' — like "**p**" in *paper*

s — like "**s**" in *sun*

ts, ts' — like the "**ts**" sound at the end of *cats*

ty, ty' — like "**t**" in *tune*

u — *like "***ew***" in chew*

w — like "**w**" in *wash*

x — like "**sh**" in *shovel*

y — like "**y**" in *yam*

' — a glottal stop, like the brief catch in the throat in *uh-oh*

Consonants marked with an **apostrophe (')** are called ejectives and are pronounced like the regular sound, but more sharply, with a popping push of air.

The first line of "Chajk," "Mi jk'ajtyiñ ap'ätyälel, chajk" is pronounced *mee hk'ahteen ap'etaylayl chahk.*

Chajk

Lend me your strength.
I am flame born from lightning's strike.
Take from me what I will never know.
Understand me.
Ask for me with a breath of wind.
I am not like the sky,
eternal.
While I sleep, I am searching
for the birth of my voice.

chajk — lightning

Chajk

Mi jk'ajtyiñ ap'ätyälel, chajk
joñoñ ik'äk'aloñ xu'chajk,
lok'sabeñoñ jiñi machbä tyajbilik.
Ña'tyañoñku.
K'ajtyibeñoñku yik'oty iwujtyaj jiñi ik'.
Mach joñoñik,
jiñi pañchañ machbä añik ityamlel,
woli ksäklañ tyi wäyel,
iyilo' pañumil kty'añ.

I

My Language

i

My language is the constellations,
fireflies in the dark.
My language is yellow corn, *k'äñk'äñ ixim*, new to the world
turning to blue, *chäkchab*, as it becomes.
My language is tilled, wet earth
where games of butterflies are born.

If I could describe the happiness of my language,
I would with flowers, belled and white.
If I could unwrap its wounds, I would do so
in times of cold, so that our bones embraced.

Kty'añ

i

Jiñi kty'an che' bajche' ek'tyak mi imos jiñi pañchañ,
che' bajche' xk'äjk'äs yäpyäpña che' ik'yoch'añ.
jiñi kty'añ che' bajche' k'äñk'äñ ixim che' mi ilok'el tyi pañumil,
chäkchab ixim mi isujtyel che' mi yochel tyi ap'ätyälel.
Ili kty'añ ach'päk'añbä lum ya' baki mi ityejchel iyälas
xpejpemtyak.

Muk'ikax imejlel kts'ijbubeñ ityijikñäyel ili kty'añ
Mi kmel yik'oty xpapañichim,
muk'ikax imejlel pits'chokoñ ilojwel ili kty'añ,
mi kmel che' tyi yoralel tsäñal cha'an che' jiñi mi imek'ob ibäj
lakbäkel.

They ask me about my language, how it is made,
I tell them they should carry a pitcher to the creek.

They want to know about this wailing,
I tell them to walk in a place of rocks.

Smoke streams from the house
where the spirit of our language lives,
where its pieces are preserved.

Sown into the soil, our language flourishes.
Washed by water, it moves like a rainbow.

But now, the sounds are distant, unclear,
My language waits, burying itself in the dirt.

Spoken, my language emits joy,
a love yet to be touched, difficult music,
the first kiss from a cunning heart.

ii

Mi ik'ajtyibeñoñob cha'añ imejlib ili kty'añ,
mi ksubeñob cha'añ la'ikuchob jiñi uk'um tyi pa'.

Mi ik'ajtyibeñoñob cha'añ isoñil jiñi äjakñabä,
mi ksubeñob cha'añ mi icha'leñob xämbal tyi xajlelol.

Iyejtyal ili kty'añ tyi otyoty ba'jupukña jiñi buts'
ya'baki lotyol tyi chajp tyi chajp kty'añlojoñ.

Mi ipäjk'el tyi lum kty'añlojoñ cha'añ mi ip'ojlel,
tyi pa' mi ipojkel cha'añ mi iñijkañ ibäj kajche' ty'oxja'.

Mach tsikilik wäle ityiwtyiwñäyel ili kty'añ
mukul chumul tyi xujk, mi ipijtyañ ibäj tyi malil lum.

Ili kty'añ che' mi icha'leñ ty'añ mi ilok'sañ tyijikñajaxbä,
ya' tyi iñäk' mi ilok'sañ k'uxbiyaj maxtyobä tyälbilik,
jiñäch machbä tyälbilik k'ay yik'oty ñaxañbä ts'ujts'uyaj tyi ityojlel
chañchañbä pusik'al.

My language brings the feeling of rain
sometimes like dew,
sometimes a downpour.
Other days, it is quiet,
losing itself in the shallows of a stream.
Suddenly, my language appears again
like the mockingbird in times of longing.

Crack of thunder in June,
gusts in the dark, my language asks—
how is the world?
My language becomes power, lightning, the sun.

iii

Ili kty'añ mi ich'äñ tyilel iyujts'il ja'al,
tyajol ye'eb,
tyajol kolem ja'al,
yambä k'iñ ñäch'äkña,
xityikotyol mi isäty ibäj tyi imalil pa',
mi itsuk' tyilel, mi icha' tyilel che' bajche' ts'uñuñtyak
che' tyi yoralel pijtyayaj.

Ili kty'añ che' bajche' xu'chajk che' tyi juño,
che' bajche' ju'ukñabä ik' che' ik'tyo,
mi ik'ajtyiñ bajche' añ iyejtyal tyi pañumil,
mi isujtyel tyi ch'ejl, mi isujtyel tyi chajk, mi isujtyel tyi k'iñ.

Dragonflies

Iridescence floating, naked
wings murmur.
Dragonflies warm them-

selves, laughing
behind twilight's back
in a sphere of fire.

xTyuluxtyak

Jiñi xtyuluxtyak che'bä ibojñib bajche' ty'oxja' mi ik'elob ibäj tyi ik',
Che' jäpäkñayob tyi ichañlel p'its'iltyak iwich',
Tyi ixojoblel k'iñ mi ityikwesañob ibäj.

Jiñi xk'äjk'äs tse'tse'ña tyi ipaty ak'lel yik'oty iwoxwox k'ajk.

Fire

What remains of the fire gleams.
In morning's frost, I don't know
how to coax the flames.
Lunging at me, then cackling,
the fire burns and my hands stir the coals.

K'ajk

Jiñjach xkälel che' jerjerña jiñi k'ajk,
k'ajk'ajña itse'tyañoñ,
cha'añ mach kujilik xik'ol che' tyi tsuwañ säk'ajel,
che' mi kputyuñ xik' järjärña mi ichuk,
jiñi k'ajk mi yajñel che' jiñi jk'äb mi ixik'.

Ichtyeja'

Let me dive into your murky green,
the water slapping your rocks.
Let me enter with slow steps, numb,
mouth mute, as I sink into your depths.

Let me lose myself among the *puyil*,
my throat wet with breath.
Fill my fragile body with wind,
and I will drift through the debris.

Ichtyeja' — a river in Tumbalá, Mexico
puyil — a type of snail found in Chiapas

Ichtyeja'

Ichtyeja',
ak'eñon ktyop' jiñi yäxty'ulañbä awa'lel,
jiñi tyuñuja' ty'uñlawbä ya' tyi awa'al,
ak'ä tyi ochel k'uñtye'bä kok, tsäñäwujulbä kwuty,
yik'oty ili ktyi' x-uma'bä cha'añ mi isul ibäj tyi añäk'.

Ak'äyoñ tyi sajtylel tyi apuyil,
ak'ä kbik' cha'añ mi isul ibäj tyi ajap ik',
ak'ä ili k'uñlikañbä kbäk'tyal mi ibujty'el tyi awik'il
cha'añ che' jiñi kmejlel tyi xämbal tyi tsuklel.

Glimmerings

I am silent in the depths of thought,
shattering when there are glimmers, flickers,
a smile and rain on the wings of the wind.
My voice unsteady, beneath the shelter of an immense sky.

Alä tsäñlawbä

Ñäch'äloñ tyi ityamlel kña'tyibal,
ch'ixikñayoñ che' ts'äylaw lemlaw,
joñoñ tse'tse'ñayoñ yik'oty ja'al tyi iwich' jiñi ik'.
Jiñi kty'añ tsiltsilña tyi imosil kolem pañchañ.

Whispers

During the rainy season, I hear the toads' song.
In muddied water, like lovers under a full moon,
they whisper, watching each other closely.

xPokoktyak

Yoralel ja'al, ik'ay jiñi xpokok ya' tyi ok'ol ja',
ju'ukñajax che' bajche' muk'bä ik'uxbiñob ibäj che' pomol uj
woli imuku subeñob ibäj ya' tyi lämäl ja' mi iyojch'oñob ibäj.

Earth's Gift

This body lets go of the night's breeze,
and my soul, allegory of space,
stands naked before time,
a gift from you.

Imajtyañ lum

Jiñi kbäk'tyal mi ibu'lichañ iyik'il ak'lel,
jiñi kch'ujlel jiñäch iyejtyal ajñibäl:
añoñ tyi ityojlel tyamlel,
kpits'lel jiñäch imajtyañ ili lum.

I Belong to the Night

Cloaked by darkness,
I hide with quavering voice.
The night is awake,
watches me,
comes to take me.
My words slip, my veins fill
with new blood. Warmed,
I belong to the night.

Icha'añoñ ak'lel

Jiñi ak'lel woli ibäk'oñ tyi ipislel.
Mi kputs'tyañ kbäj tyi itsiltsilñäyel kty'añ.
Jiñi ak'lel kañal iwuty,
woli ityul k'eloñ,
tsa' tyili ipäyoñ majlel,
ktyi' mi ibujty'el tyi ma'ma' ty'añ,
kchijil mi ibujty'el tyi tsijib ch'ich',
ma'añik tsäñal, icha'añoñ ak'lel.

 ◇◇◇

Freshwater Spring

In the evening, I beat at the silence
with a steady voice. I shout—
I am a woman!
Freshwater spring, source of my existence.

Yäxty'ulañbä iya'lel kajñibal

Tyi tsuwañbä ik'ajel, mi ityuk' iñäch'tyälel,
Jiñäch k'uñtye' mi ksub:
x-ixikoñäch,
woli ktyaj yäxty'ulañbä iya'lel kajñibal tyi pañumil.

Sacred Mother

Under a full moon,
air brushes my skin.
I don't want my wounds to bleed
nor my spirit to weep.
Now, in the white beam of our Sacred Mother,
my discovery.

Ch'ujulbä kña'

Jiñäch ak'lel pomol uj,
Ili tsuwañ ik' mi ityajpuñ kpächälel,
Mach komik käk' tyi lok'el ich'ich'el ili lojwel
mi jiñik iyuk'el kch'ujlel,
jiñ cha'añ mi käk' kbäj tyi ityojlel tyi isäkpomälel ik'äk'al
lakch'ujuña',
Jiñäch wäle, mi isujtyel ktyaj kbäj.

  ◇◇◇

Prayer for a Teacher

In memory of José Antonio Reyes Matamoros

Fallen body,
let me hold you in death and raise you up.
My uncertain fingers find you.
In your memory—
may I return
like the peaceful spirit
that brings air, fire, daybreak and life.
I want to echo you in the world.

Ch'ujul ty'añ

Cha'añ iña'tyäñtyel José Antonio Reyes Matamoros

Ch'ujulbä k'ay cha'añ abäk'tyal yajlemixbä,
mi kch'äm achämel mi kñuk-esañety,
tsiltsilña iyal jk'äbtyak mi ktyajety,
cha'añ aña'tyäñtyel:
Kom sujtyel;
che'bajche' tyijikñabä pañumil
muk'bä yäk' säkjamtyäl, ik', k'ajk yik'oty kuxtyälel.
Kom ixojobleloñ aty'añ tyi pañumil.

I Am Here

I am here with few words, fallen
like *ktatuch* in the time of hunting.
I am here searching for peace
to heal my torn mouth,
smell the cooking fires,
coax song from my lips.
I am here to dig into betrayal, to drown
myself in what eats at my words.
Here, in this wild land,
I will dance for years to come.

ktatuch – my grandfather

Wä'añoñ ilayi

Wä' añoñ ilayi yik'oty juñp'ajl cha'p'ajl ty'añ yajleñtyakixbä,
che' bajche' tsa' yäsabeyob ibäk'tyal ktatuch che' yoralel ajñel tyi
matye'el,
wä'añoñ ilayi woli ksäklañ ñäch'tyälel cha'añ mi imejlel kläw ili
ktyi' tsijlembä,
cha'añ mi imejlel kubibeñ iyujts'il jiñi pulembä lew,
cha'añ mi imejlel kletsañ k'ay tyi ktyi',
wä'añoñ ilayi cha'añ mi imejlel kpikbeñ ich'ujlel jiñi k'el wuty,
cha'añ mi kts'aj kbäj ya' tyi ixojoblel muk'bä ik'ux kak',
ila tyi matye'lum mi kloty kbäk'tyal
cha'añ muk'tyo kbej cha'leñ soñ tyi ityojlel jabilel.

My Body

Immense world,
my body is your creation—
deep as the color of leaves,
steady, strong as the branches.
Trembling, you take me in.

Acha'añ kbäk'tyal

Kolem lum,
acha'añ kbäk'tyal
yäx-elañ che' bajche' ayopol
xuk'ul che' bajche' tsätsbä itye',
tsiltsilña kch'ujlel, mi ach'ämoñ.

Footprints

Cold earth,
I live in your blood,
an intelligent woman
who walks lightly through the world.

Kyejtyal

Itsäñälel klum
mi achumtyañ ach'ich'el
che' bajche' p'ip'bä x-ixik
mi käsiñ ty'uchtyañ majlel pañumil.

Dance of the Rain

What does the world do in night's cold
when the *puyil* sing to the dance of the rain?

In February, loneliness appears
like an orphan, secretly,
announcing forgottenness.

In May, I see the rain dance
under the clouds,
the world darkening with desire
to shed its anger.

Again, the rain dances.
My life is fleeting,
and my thoughts solitary.
Tears fall from the sky into the fire,
lightning's ax wounds.
This is how it is,
and me, I dance for the rain,
to hear the beating of my heart.

puyil — a type of snail found in Chiapas

Isoñil ja'al

¿Chuki mi imel jiñi pañumil che' tyi tsuwañ ak'lel
che' muk' tyi k'ay puy tyi ityojlel isoñil ja'al?

Mi kubiñ tyi soñ ja'al che' tyi pebrero,
ñäch'äl mi ityilel tyi kbajñelil,
ch'ijiyem mi ityilel che' me'ba' jiñi ch'ujlel,
o che' yomjach imuku sub ñajäyel.

Tsa' jk'ele tyi soñ ja'al che' tyi mayo,
mäkäkña, mich'ikña,
ik'tyokañbä pañumil, weñ yom uk'el yilal,
che' bajche' yom ichokbeñ imich'ajel jiñi ik'.

Mi jk'el tyi soñ ja'al,
ñumeljachbä k'uxtyälel,
Pits'ilbä bajñal ña'tyayaj,
tyi yojlil its'äbts'äbñäyel k'ajk,
mi yajlel iwuty jiñi ja'al tyi ktyojlel,
mi iyajlel jiñi jacha chajk tyi ipam lum,
muk' tyi low, muk' tyi mil,
añkese che'ächi, mi ksoñiñ ja'al yik'oty its'äbts'äbñäyel kpusik'al.

II

Ancestors

There, in the forest of quetzales, sound of dry wood falling,
the ancestors' song is whispered in thunder,
fire's tongue coats the world.

As the sun dies, our Sacred Mother is born,
the grandmothers beg for quiet.
Gathering themselves for the dance of the forest,
they are guardians of ritual.

Our grandmothers are calling, making requests
for those who have been silenced—
the invisible, dead, raped and burnt in secret.

The women fill the air with incense.
Trees bow, a stream surges,
and their power unites.

Chuchu'bälob

Ya' tyi ch'ujulbä we'tye' icha'añ ñukbä matye'el icha'añ k'uk'wits
käñlaw ity'añob yik'oty wälwälñayob mi yälob jiñi ch'ujul k'ay tyi
ty'añ mamäl,
iyak' k'ajk mi iletsel tyi pañumil che' bajche' uts'atybä k'ay.

Che' mi ichämel jiñi k'iñ, che' mi yilañ pañumil jiñ lakch'ujuña',
jiñi chuchu'bälob mi ik'ajtyiñob ñäch'tyälel,
jiñjach ijäjäk'ayob mi ikomob ibäj isoñil matye'el
yik'oty iyumob cha'añ oño'ch'ujutyesayaj.

Jiñi chuchu'bälob muk'ob tyi pay, woliyob tyi wokol ty'añ, mi
imelob k'ajtyiyaj,
icha'añ jiñi machbä muk'ik iyäjk'elob tyi ty'añ,
icha'añob machbä tsikilobik tsäñsäbilobä tyik'läbilobä yik'oty
mukul pulemobä.

Woli iletsañob jiñi pom, woli ibuts'iñob ch'ujulbä ajñibäl
jiñi ik' woli iñumel, jiñi ja' yolyolña woli iñumel,
che' jiñi pejtyelel p'ätyälel mi ikomob ibäj tyi jump'ej ch'ujlel.

X-ixik

Time is yours, *x-ixik*,
embroidering your body with pain.
Like stone to chisel, you give yourself up,
bathe in the sharp fragrance of incense,
so that your strength will not run out.

The years imprint your skin.
Mother Earth is our goodness, our world.
Our roots remain within the caves.
Scent of candle wax
and a diminishing fire—
this is our loneliness, *x-ixik*, our origin.

x-ixik — woman

X-ixik

Acha'añäch ili tyamlel, x-ixik
mi ajoch' majlel abäk'tyal yik'oty k'uxel
mi awäk' abäk'tyal che' bajche' melbilbä xajlel
che' bajche' mi aboñ abäj tyi yujts'il pom
cha'añ ma'añik mi jilel ap'ätyälel.

Jiñi tyamlel mi ijoch' majlel abäk'tyal,
jiñi lakña' lum jiñäch iweñlel, jiñäch lakpañumil.
Iyejtyal tsa'bä käle tyi imal ch'eñ
lotyol icha'añ iyujts'il pom
yik'oty ixuch'il ñichim,
Jiñäch lakbajñelil, jiñäch lakajñib. X-ixik.

 ❖❖❖

Chuchu’

Chuchu’, I rest in your heart.
Thoughts of the *kaxlañ* were strangling me, devouring me,
then your spirit came like an afternoon storm.
You are of the forest, you belong to it.
My soul shudders,
my body becomes lightning.

chuchu’ — grandmother
kaxlañ — non-Indigenous, from *castellano* ‘Spanish’

Chuchu’

Tsa’ jk’aja ko’ tyi apusik’al kchuchu’,
jiñi kaxlañ ña’tyibal woli imiloñ, woli its’u-oñ.
Che’ jiñi tsa’ tyili ach’ujlel bajche’ lakmam:
Jatyety ipäk’ilety matye’el, icha’añety
ch’ixikña kch’ujlel tsa’ majli,
kbäk’tyal ta’ sujtyi che’ bajche’ chajk.

This Land, Your World

The candle sits undisturbed,
smoldering pine in the air,
and a memory of you travels through time.
It is your presence in my song, *Chuchu'*.

chuchu' — grandmother

Jiñäch ili lum apañumil

Ma'añik ñijkäbil ixuch'il ñichim
Lotyol icha'añ ixojokñäyel jiñi pom
Jiñi lum apañumiläch
Aña'tyäñtyel añ tyi tyamlel
Awajñibäch tyi jk'ay, chuchu'.

 ❖❖❖

Tatuch

Walls of this house witness
your work sewn by time,
past and future together.
Your language, its wisdom, in this soil.
Here, your song continues.
Your name, your spirit—
in the walls of this house,
your words and prayers live.

tatuch — grandfather

Tatuch

Tatuch ipaty ili ñoxi' otyoty,
tsa' ik'eleyety,
jiñäch tyamlel woli its'is awe'tyel,
ñumeñixbä, wolibä iyujtyel mi ikälel,
iyutslel aty'añ ila tyi lum.
Ilayi, añ ip'ätyälel ak'ay
ak'aba, aty'añ awejtyal,
ilayi, tyi ipaty ili otyoty, tatuch
wä'chumul asuboñel yik'oty ach'ujulty'añ.

X-Askuñ

Bells chime in the church
of the Archangel Saint Michael.
You fill the casket, and the faces of the women
answer in agony.

It has been three months since you drove away.
You took our ancestors' satchel, sodden with smoke,
so many years hanging on the wooden post.
Sadness was in your face, even though you smiled.

Now, in your casket, uprooted and torn from life,
I think this is a nightmare, I want to wake up.
I think you are breathing.
I think you will return to drink your pozol.
You are going to come back, a handful of greens
and fistful of chiles in your bag.

X-Askuñ, X-Askuñ, you travelled
in a dream, brief life.
Now, my tears overflow this bowl.
X-Askuñ, X-Askuñ, I will drink slowly,
so I will not search for the path you walked.

x-askuñ — older brother
pozol — fermented corn drink

 ◇◇◇

X-Askuñ

Tsiñtsiña jiñi uxlujump'ej ijats'o tya'k'iñ
ya' tyi yotyotylel ch'ujutyesayaj Sañ Mikel Arkankel,
awajñib ik'woxañ ya' baki ñolol abäk'tyal,
jiñi iwutyob x-ixikob woli ijak'ob yoj.

Uxp'ej uw che' tsa' majliyety, tsa' jk'eleyety tsa' letsiyety ya' tyi ñoxi'
xäñibal,
tsa' ach'ämä majlel ichim lakñojtye'el,
jiñi ñoxi' chim añixbä ibuts'il wajalixbä jok'ol ya' tyi ñoxi' oy,
ya' tyi awuty añ ts'itya' ch'ijiyemlel, tse'ekña atyi'.

Wäle abäk'tyal che'jax bajche' tyomel tye' añety tyi awajñib,
mi kña'tyañ cha'añ ñajaljach, kom mi ijajmel kwuty,
mi kña'tyañ cha'añ woli ajap ik',
mi kña'tyañ cha'añ tyalety ajap asa',
cha'añ mi ikajel ajulel yik'oty juñbuts apimel tyi ak'äb,
yik'oty juñjojp ich tyi achim.

X-Askuñ, X-Askuñ, tsa' ñumiyety tyi ñajal machbä jocholik,
machbä tyamik,
jiñjach wäle juñjojp uk'el machbä ochik tyi tsimaj,
X-Askuñ, X-Askuñ, abu'lich lum, awa'al lum, mi ikajel kjape' tyi
jujup'is.

Death Bed

Laid out on the palm mat,
eyes twitching,
ichtyo' wets your mouth.
Destiny has silenced you,
turned your heart like a new moon.
You were sacrificed to the cave's darkness.

ichtyo' — a type of pepper used for medicinal purposes

Ñoxi' pojp

Abäk'tyal ya'añ tyi ñoxi' pojp,
ty'ulty'ulña awuty,
juñbujk' ichtyo' mi yäch'esañ atyi',
jiñi ñajtylel tsa' iñäch'tyesa aty'añ,
tsa' paj-esäñtyi apusik'al che' tsijib uj,
ach'ujlel tsa' majtyañ ak'eñtyi ik'yoch'añbä ch'eñ.

Damp, Turned Earth

In the dark, an owl opens the door to sadness,
dances where your corpse was tossed,
drinks your pain, laughs behind a black cloak.
Dense fog surrounds you beneath a dead moon,
shadows slice your limbs.
A curse killed your spirit.
Ity'äñty'äñäyel, the sound of one day,
and your death, like the smell of damp, turned earth.

ity'äñty'äñäyel — an onomatopoeic word that mimics a heartbeat
in its repetition of the root *ty'äñ*

Iyujts'il ach'päk'añbä lum

Jiñi xku, tyi yojilil ak'lel mi ijam ityi' yotyotylel ch'ijiyemlel,
muk' tyi soñ ya' baki xipil abäk'tyal,
woli ijap ak'uñtye' aj-ajñäyel, woli itsetyañety tyi ipaty ak'lel,
tyi pukjubeñbä tyokal mi ichokety tyi yojlil chämeñbä
lakch'ujuña',
kolem xojoblel mi ibik'tyi tsep abäk'tyal.
Juñp'ajl ty'añ tyik'läbilbä tsa' itsäñesa ach'ujlel,
ity'äñty'äñäyel jump'ejbä k'iñ ichämel akuxtyälel,
Che' iyujts'il bajche' ach'päk'añbä lum.

A Mother's Heart

Caught in silence,
my wounds bare to the trees,
how many months must my heart carry?
How many rains must I wait?
The winter comes suddenly, demanding to know of death.
Surround me with the sweet incense of our ancestors.
Let the fire's flames soften my cries,
a mother's heart is bigger than death.

Ipusik'al ña'äl

Jiñi iyejtyal alojwel che' bajche' tyambä ik'ajel icha'añ añäch'tyälel,
che' bajche' jochkälañbä matye'el jiñi alojwel,
¿Jayp'ej uw mi ikajel iläty' apusik'al?
¿Jayp'ej ja'al mi ikajel apijtyañ?
Kome jiñi tsäñal weñ mich' tyal mi ikajel ik'ajtyiñ achämel.
Ak'eñoñ kbuts'iñety tyi tsajakñabä pom icha'añ lakñojtye'elob
la' ñäch'esañ iyuk'el apusik'al yik'oty ik'äk'al ak'ajk,
läty'ä, kome jiñi apusik'al cha'añ ña'äl ñumeñ ñuk bajche' chämel.

Your Birth

The sky painted itself white.
My heart welcomed you
between pain and numbness,
tears fell from my eyes.
I didn't recognize myself,
only saw you, touched you, enjoyed you.
I showed you to *Ch'ujutyaty*,
He held your small body.
Ch'ujutyaty blessed your spirit,
and since then, He has watched over you.

Ch'ujutyaty — sacred father

Che' tsa' awila pañumil

Che' tsa' awila pañumil, aläl, tsa' iboño ibä pañchañ tyi säsäk.
Ibajñelbä kpusik'al tsa' ich'ämäyety,
tyi jk'uxel yik'oty jseñlel
tsa' yajli iya'lel kwuty ñajtybä añ,
ma'añik tsa' jkäñ käñä kbä,
tsa' jk'eleyety, tsa' ktyäläyety, tsa' ktyijikñesa kbä tyi atyojlel,
tsa' kpäsäyety tyi lakch'ujutyaty,
Ch'ujutyaty tsa' imek'e awalä bäk'tyal
Ch'ujutyaty tsa' imoso ach'ujlel,
k'äläl che' jiñi, Ch'ujutyaty mi ikañ iwuty.

 ◇◇◇

Girl

Asleep like the day's light,
rigid in the dawn, I see you laugh,
even though you are in pain.
When was I silenced and lost you?
And whose hands helped me to lift your small body
that disappeared like the white flowers?

xCh'ok

Awuty wäyäl che' tyi ik'äk'al k'iñil,
tsuwañ mi itsil abäk'tyal che' bajche' säk'ajel,
mi kñajleñ cha'añ woli atse'tyañoñ che' woliyety tyi bajk'el.
¿Chuki tyi k'iñil tsa' ñäch'iyoñ yik'oty tsa' ksätyäyety?
¿Majki tsa' iñusa ik'äb ya' tyi awalä bäk'tyal
wolijaxtyobä ijajwel bajche' säsäk ñichim?

Healer

The healer mixes herbs, fragrance
for my spirit and self—
greenness of epazote
clarity of mint, fear's cure,
yellow of the marigold
black incense
white camphor.
These clear my way in the world.
The healer turns her face to the sun,
our creator,
and asks a favor.
From her lips, sacred words of protection
spoken for new creation.
Aroma of leaves around my steps,
and this, my healer, interpreter and cure.

epazote — also known as wormseed or Mexican tea,
an aromatic herb with a pungent flavor

Xwujty

Jiñäch xwujty mi ixäk'e' iyujts'il jiñi yopotye',
cha'añ kbäk'tyal yik'oty kch'ujlel.
Iyäxty'ulañlel jiñi xpasoñtye',
Iyäxmajañlel jiñi ts'äkal bäk'eñ,
Ik'añjuch'äñlel iñich xtyijol,
yik'muläñlel jiñi pom,
isäsäklel jiñi x-alcanpor
jiñäch iyujts'iltyak muk'bä ijam kbijlel tyi pañumil.
Jiñäch xwujty mi iletsañ ity'añ tyi ityojlel ch'ujultyaty tsa'bä mele
iñi' kolem lum,
Mi ik'ajtyiñ tyi wokol ty'añ kñumib,
mi ilok'sañ tyi ityi' ch'ujulbä ty'añ tyi ktyojlel,
käñtyayaj, yejtyal weñ ach'tyobä,
tsijib päk'embä cha'añ yambä ch'ok-ayaj.
Jiñäch itsajakñäyel yopotye'tyak mi ik'el majlel kok,
jiñäch xwujty, kñusaj-ty'añ jts'äkayaj.

Bewitched

Cry of a star,
evening's silence,
stark. I pass the hours,

small piece of the world, the day
round, shadows seeking
the masked.

What is the work of memory
in the night? What is the point
of anything when the forest soothes,
bewitches?

Mi isätyoñ

Päk'äl tyi ktyojlel iyuk'el ek',
Uts'atybä ñäch'tyälel tyi jochkälañbä ik'ajel,
Tyajol mi kñumel.

Ipäk'iloñ abäk'tyal,
ya' baki selel jiñi k'iñ.
Ixojoblel k'iñil mi isäklañ lotyolbä.

Chuki ye'tyel kcha'añ jiñi lotyolbä
jiñi ak'lel wä'añ yik'otyoñ,
chuki ye'tyel kcha'añ tyi ipejtyelel
jiñi matye'el mi ilaj ak'eñoñ yik'oty mi isätyoñ.

 ◇◇◇

I Am the Night

Scent of wind,
my body, a dream
as the fire burns down.

Ak'leloñ

Joñoñ ak'leloñ iyujts'il ik',
kbäk'tyal jiñäch ñajal
che' wolix ijilel jiñi k'ajk.

III

Chechebak

Show your face,
let me breathe your stale aroma.
I need to know where you are,
so that I understand
when you will come for me.
In bed, worry gnaws and I wake,
sweating, gasping.
I understand your scorn.
You come to me in a dream
but are invisible. I sense your laughter,
hovering between love and derision.

chechebak — skeletal

Chechebak

Komkatsa' jk'el bajche' yilalety,
komkatsa' kubiñ bajche' yubil awujts'il,
mi kp'is atyamlel cha'añ mi kña'tyañ baki tyilelety,
kome mach tsikilik mi atyilel tyi ktyojlel,
ili k'oj-ob mi ityik'lañoñ che' ik'yoch'añ mi kjam kwuty
mi ktyaj ili kbäk'tyl ach'päk'añ tyi tsuwañ bu'lich,
woswosña kjap ik', mi ich'ämbeñ isujm tyi kña'tyibal bajche'
yilalety,
jik'jik'ñajach atse'tyañoñ mi asujtyel che' tyam kwäyel,
mach käñäletyik mi atyilel, jiñjach mi kubiñ atse'eñal che' bajche'
k'uxbiyaj
yik'oty che' bajche' säsäk tse'eñal.

I Refuse

No longer ornament for your silence,
my smile will not get you off.
I will not be silent
in the violence of your mornings.
I hide myself and will not help
you hurt my body.
I will be the moon's path,
where the wind will reveal the day.

Mi kmuk

Mi kmuk kbäj, cha'añ mach komix ichäñ ch'äliboñ añäch'tyälel,
cha'añ mach komix ichäñ tse'ekñäyeloñ atyikwälel,
mach komix chäñ ñäch'äl cha'añ joñtyolbäl asäk'ajel,
mi kmuk kbäj cha'añ mach komix kchäñ koltyañety cha'añ mi
ayäx-esañ kbäk'tyal,
kom wäle cha'añ ibijleloñ ak'lel ya' baki jiñi ik' mi iñumel tyi
päsibal k'iñ.

Disappearance

You disappear.
In the forest, you swim
through the dusk and dirt.
You dream of money falling into your hands,
your words falter.

Ik' yik'oty ik'yoch'äyel

Jiñi abäk'tyal mi isujtyel tyi lojk tyileñumelbä
tyi imalil matye'el yik'oty ya' baki tyo'ol pits'ilbä lum,
woliyety tyi ñuxujel tyi ik'tyak yik'oty ik'yoch'äyel
mi añajleñ jiñi tya'k'iñ che' mi ikajel tyi yajlel tyi ak'äb
mi awälwäl al juñp'ajl ty'añ tyi alujbel.

Flight

From your mouth faint voices,
a distant chorus. Your pleas
are caught by the wind,
like the wren flying past
in these times of fear.

Iwejlib ts'uñuñ

Jiñi wälwälñabä atyi' melbilbä tyi lajchämp'ej ty'añ tyilembä tyi
ñajtylel,
jiñi jak'oj che'bä bajche' sasak'aytyak,
jok'ol tyi ik' mi ik'otyel tyi kchikiñ,
che'jax bajche' ipäm wejlel ts'uñuñ ili yoralel bäbäk'eñbä.

This Road

Not straight, maybe curved,
sometimes obscured,
raw then searing.
You might be hungry or thirsty.

The path is difficult, and you hide yourself
from the coyote who is hungry
for the loneliness that has taken root
in your mind.
Worries of survival circle,
time does not pause, will not stop.

Your eyes open, the possibility of sleep has vanished,
dreaming is not the way to another home.

Abijlel

Mach jäxälik iyejtyal awok,
añ ityajol ts'otyiktyik, añ ityajol mäkäkña,
añ ityajol tsuwañ, tyikwal,
tyi yañtyakbä k'iñ wi'ñal yik'oty tyikiñ ityi'.

Wokoljax abijlel mi aloty abäj cha'añ ma'añik mi ityajety jiñi
xmatye' ts'i',
wi'ñal tyi atyojlel, tyi abajñelil,
abajñelil muk'bä isujtyel che' bajche' xajlel tyi aña'tyibal,
ity'äñty'äñäyel abäk'tyal mi ijijtyel tyi tyamlel,
tyamlel machbä añik ijäxtyälel, ma'añik mi iwa'tyäl.

Awuty mi ik'el iwejlib k'aj-oj machbä añik ibijlel,
ñajal wejlib ma'añik iñumib tyi yambä lum.

Evidence

You will not be able to hide what's left—
promises drowned by rivers,
the untold kept underground.
Their music remains in the mountains,
in the *wäy* disguised as Jaguar, Gray Fox, Snake.
You will not forget,
but remembering will suffocate you.

wäy — personal guardian spirit that takes the form of an animal

Ña'tyayaj

Ma'añik mi ikajel imejlel alaj muk pejtyelel iyejtyal oño' xämbal,
p'ujp'ubil jiñi ty'añ ya' tyi pa'tyak,
mukbil jiñi lotybilbä ty'añ tyi lum,
käylem ikäñlawlel k'ay ya' tyi ichañlel matye'el
ya' baki mosol ich'ujlel oño' wäyob,
ma'añik mi ikajel iñajäyel acha'añ iwelwelñäyel ak'ajtyesaj,
jiñi ak'ajtyesaj mi ikajel imil awik'.

Vultures

Vultures wait for you at the road's turn
in the unbearable heat of the day.
They wait for you,
your eyes dim with hunger.
The vultures search for your footprints
where anxiety grows.
Steps lost in dry leaves,
you are unmoored
and the vultures wait for you,
the crumbs of your life.

xTya'jolob

Jiñi xtya'jolob machbä añik mi ityajob iñaj-añ, mi ipijtyañetyob
ya' tyi xäk' bij
che' weñ tsäts ityikwälel k'iñ,
jiñi xtya'jolob mi ichijtyañ awuty tyok'tyok'tyakixbä cha'añ lujbel
yik'oty wi'ñal,
wi'ñal tsa'ixbä iyaj-esa abäk'tyal,
jiñi xtya'jolob mi itsäklañ awok ya' tyi yambä lum,
ya' tyi lum ya'baki mi ip'ojlel jak'-oj,
jiñi k'uñlikanixbä awok mi isajtyel majlel tyi tyikiñ yopotye',
che'ety bajche' jukub machbä añik ilujkujib,
jiñi xtya'jolob wolix ipijtyañetyob cha'añ mi ik'uxob iyujtyibal
ity'äñty'äñäyel akuxtyälel.

Dreaming Undocumented

You are learning to walk on time's path
while swallows watch from the caves.
Secretly, you enter the mouth of another land,
fog blanketing a naked earth.

Ik'pukambä ñajal

Joñoñ juñtyikil machbä añik ijuñ wolibä iñop iñusañ yajñib tyamlel,
xwilistyak mi ik'eloñ tyi majlel kome yujil cha'añ
muk'jach ikajel kmuku ñumel ya' tyi ityi' yambä lum che'bä bajche'
ik'pukambä ñajal muk'bä imuk kälel jiñi pits'ilbä lum.

Muted

In a country that is not yours, there is no light.
You live in foreign speech. You exist,
muted and silent.

Uma' ñäch'tyälel

Che' mi ichumtyäñtyel lum machbä lakcha'añik, ma'añik ak'lel,
ma'añik k'iñil,
che' mi lakchumtyañ yambä juñp'ajl ty'añ tyi lum machbä
lakcha'añik,
muk'jach lakpejkañ x-uma' ñäch'tyälel.

What You Have Lived Through

These new waters
created from rhythm and symbol,
a dream at dusk.
This poem turns into dawn.

Lush and verdant mountain,
tender hummingbird,
share what you have lived through.

Ak'eñõñ achumtyäbal

Ixä tsijibä ñoj pa'
Tyejchbilbä tyi soñ yik'oty iyejtyal
jiñäch kñajal tyi yik'añ
jiñäch ñichty'añ muk'bä isujtyel tyi säk'ajel.

Yäxty'ulañbä kolem matye'wits
lichikña ts'uñuñ
ak'eñoñ achumtyäbal.

 ◇◇◇

Time Passing

Sturdy mountain, I give myself to you.
Protect me in your shadows,
so that I won't falter when I speak.
Wrap my thoughts in water.
Come, so that I may travel on a path beyond time.

Iñumelal tyamlel

Mi käk'eñety kbäj p'ätyälbä matye'el
Mosoyoñ tyi axojoblel
Cha'añ mach mi kyajlel che' mi ktyech kty'añ
Bäk'ä ili kña'tyibal yik'oty awa'lel,
ak'eñoñ awajñibal cha'añ mi kñusañ majlel tyamlel.

Poetry's Silence

Like how rum is drunk, sip by sip,
or how a dance is understood
when there is nothing left in time's glass.

Jap

Che' mi ijajpel iñäch'tyälel ñichty'añ
che' bajche' mi ijajpel tyi jujump'is chicha,
che' mi ijajpel iñäch'tyälel soñ,
che' bajche' mi ijajpel iputs'ib ñajtylel.

When I Wake

It is quiet
in the annona tree,
twisted and hollow,
roots grown deep into the rock.
Morning, and I hear nothing.

Itye'el k'äk'ats

Ñäch'äkña tsa' kubi che' tsa' kajñi kwuty,
ya' tyi iñoxi' itye'el k'äk'ats,
käläx ñoxix kome weñ lochityikix,
iwi' tsa'ix iñusa iye'bal xajlel tyi jaybä lum,
ili säk'ajel, jiñi ñäch'tyälel mi ik'otyel tyi ipächälel kchikiñ.

My Land

I don't want to lose myself in the city,
to live when I have not written my first verse.
Grant me these hours, lit by our people
and wake me in wildness.

Kña' matye'lum

Mach komik sajtyel ila tyi kolem tyejklum,
mach käyäyik chumtyäl che' maxtyo tyejchbilik kcha'añ ñaxambä
its'ijbal jk'ay.
Majtyañ ak'eñoñ ili ak'lel ikäk'al lakpi'älob,
Jambeñoñ kwuty tyi yojlil kña' matye'lum.

Distance

This air deepens, drumming the soul of unseen things.
My days call out like the cricket's song.

Ñajtylel

Jiñi ik' jiñäch mi ityam-esañ ityip'tyip'ñäyel ich'ujlel lotyolbä,
ik'ay jiñi sajk' jiñäch ty'äñty'äñäyel ili tyambä jk'iñil.

I Am the Alphabet

They say grass is born in the forest,
my body holds the freshness of mountains.
I have absorbed the garden's blossoming.
Skin soaked by rivers,
they say I am the alphabet.
Bright light of morning is how I show myself.

Tsolts'ijboñ

Mi yälob cha'añ ixojokñäyeloñ matye'el lok'embä ilayi,
mi yälob cha'añ itsajakñäyeloñ kolem matye'wits,
mi yälob cha'añ mi kpuk majlel ñumel itsajakñäyel xotyñup'ulbä,
mi yälob kpächälel tsajakña tyi pa',
mi yälob cha'añ tsolts'ijboñ yik'oty isäkjamtyäleloñ ili lum.
Mi yälob cha'añ joñoñäch, chä'äch mi kmulañ mel kbäj.

About the Author

Juana Karen Peñate is a poet, writer, translator, educator and cultural promoter from Emiliano Zapata, Tumbalá, Chiapas, Mexico. She has authored several books of poetry in Ch'ol with self-translations in Spanish including *Mi nombre ya no es silencio* (Coneculta 2002) and *Ipusik'al Matye'lum/Corazón de Selva*, published by Pluralia in 2013. In 2020, Peñate won the Premio de Literaturas Indígenas de América for her collection *Isoñil Ja'al/ Danza de la Lluvia*, published by the University of Guadalajara. *Ñumeñ mi kajel tyi kolel bajche' k'uxel/Voy a crecer más que el dolor* was published in 2024 by Oralibrura.

About the Translators

Carol Rose Little is an assistant professor of linguistics at the University of Oklahoma whose work centers on the Ch'ol language. She learned Ch'ol through her ongoing fieldwork beginning in 2015 in Ch'ol-speaking communities in Chiapas where she has spent extended periods over the past decade. She has also served as an interpreter for Ch'ol speakers in federal and state courts in the United States.

Charlotte Friedman is a poet, author and teacher. Her poetry has been nominated for the Pushcart Prize and Best of the Net and published in *Naugatuck River Review, Stoneboat, Quartet, Timberline* and elsewhere. She is the author of *Channeling Grace* and *The Girl Pages: A Handbook of the Best Resources for Strong, Confident, Creative Girls* (Hyperion). Friedman taught narrative medicine in the English department at Barnard College, Columbia University for ten years and in hospitals in New York and Jerusalem.

Acknowledgments

Asymptote: "Disappearance," "Fire," "This Road," "Vultures," "Muted"
Exchanges: Journal of Literary Translation: "Freshwater Spring," "Ichtyeja," "Distance," "Ancestors," "I Refuse," "Evidence," "Dreaming Undocumented"
Hayden's Ferry Review: "Dance of the Rain," "Dragonflies"
Journal of Latina Critical Feminism: "X-ixik (II)," "Your Birth"
Latin American Literature Today: "Chajk," "X-ixik (I)," "Glimmerings," "Healer"
North Dakota Quarterly: "Chuchu'," "Footprints"
On the Seawall: "My Language I, II, III," "Poetry's Silence," "X-Askuñ"
Poetry London: "Girl"
The Arkansas International: "I Am the Night," "Earth's Gift"
World Literature Today: "I Am the Alphabet," "This Land, Your World," "When I Wake"

The following poems were published in Ch'ol and Spanish (translated by the author) in *Ipusik'al Matye'lum / Corazón de Selva*, (Pluralia. Mexico, 2013): Chajk, Yäxty'ulañbä ya'lel kajñibal / Manantial de mi existencia, Ch'ujul ty'añ / Canto sagrado, Iñumelal tyamlel / Más allá del tiempo, Tsolts'ijboñ / Soy alfabeto, Kyejtyal / Mis huellas, Acha'añ kbäk'tyal / Mi cuerpo tu primicia, Imajtyañ lum / Regalo de la tierra, Icha'añoñ ak'lel / Pertenezco a la noche, Ch'ujulbä kña' / Sagrada madre, Mi isätyoñ / Me embruja, Ak'eñoñ achumtyäbal / Entrégame tu eternidad, Ñajtylel / Eternidad, X-ixik I, Chuchu', Tatuch, X-ixik II, Jiñäch ili lum apañumil / Es la tierra tu universo, Xwujty / Curandera, Alä tsäñlawbä / Breves destellos.

The remainder of the poems in this collection will be published in Ch'ol and Spanish (translated by the author) in *Isoñil Ja'al/Danza de la Lluvia* (University of Guadalajara), which won the 2020 Premio de Literaturas Indígenas de América.

Recent Books from Mayapple Press:

Bitite Vinklers, *Where the Sun Sleeps at Night*, 2026
      Paper, 86pp, $20.95
      ISBN 978-1-952781-28-5
Eleanor Lerman, *Oleander Marriage*, 2025
      Paper, 76pp, $22.95
      ISBN 978-1-952781-29-2
Joy Gaines-Friedler, *Secular Audacity*, 2025
      Paper, 68pp, $21.95
      ISBN 978-1-952781-26-1
Ellen Stone, *Everyone Wants To Keep the Moon Inside Them*, 2025
      Paper, 90pp, $21.95
      ISBN: 978-1-952781-24-7
Lisken Van Pelt Dus, *How Many Hands to Home*, 2025
      Paper, 78pp, $20.95
      ISBN: 978-1-952781-23-0
David Michael Nixon, *A Wolf Comes to My Window*, 2024
      Paper, 40pp, $18.95
      ISBN: 978-1-952781-22-3
Zilka Joseph, *Sweet Melida*, 2024
      Paper, 60pp, $19.95
      ISBN: 978-1-952781-19-3
Eleanor Lerman, *Slim Blue Universe*, 2024
      Paper, 68pp, $20.95
      ISBN: 978-1-982781-17-9
Cati Porter, *Small Mammals*, 2023
      Paper, 78pp, $19.94 plus s&h
      ISBN 978-1-952781-15-5
Eleanor Lerman, *The Game Cafe*, 2022
      Paper, 160pp, $22.95 plus s&h
      ISBN 978-1-952781-13-1
Gloria Nixon-John, *The Dark Safekeeping*, 2022
      Paper, 92pp, $19.85 plus s&h
      ISBN: 978-1-952781-11-7

For a complete catalog of Mayapple Press publications, please visit our website at *mayapplepress.com*. Books can be ordered direct from our website with secure online payment using PayPal, or by mail (check or money order). Or order through your local bookseller.